I0441204

" *ending this crisis, avoiding the next* "

Jean-Claude Schmitz

First published in October 2012

Version V3; september 2015
ISBN-13: 978-1505489170
ISBN-10: 1505489172

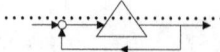

By September 15, 2008, the world got itself into a financial crisis of proportions that none of us had ever knowingly experienced, it came upon as a surprise, and left us all wondering what was going on.

The fact that by mid-2015, we have not yet recovered, but that many of us are sinking even deeper into crisis, calls for a thorough analysis of what has been and what is going on.

In the spirit of never letting a crisis to go un-used, proposals for a sounder future have to be put on the table, or, into a book like this one.

The book makes use of a few mathematical formulas here and there, the technically less inclined reader can easily skip those and stay with the text without losing track.

CONTENTS

1. Introduction

To go with Clausewitz and his comments on war and generals, I think that he last few years have shown that finance is far too serious a subject to be left to economists, politicians, or lawyers, so let a control systems engineer have a deeper look. The financial system itself does not seem to be inherently robust or stable, the optimisation of resource allocation that makes up the purpose of the financial industry is not achieved in a satisfactory manner. The optimisation of the finance sector's own income has worked a lot better.

It seems even that systematic misallocation has been the rule rather than the exception, pointing to the question as to why we need a system that serves us so badly.

One observation that could be made in the last few years was that in a world awash with debts, and in order to fight the sovereign debt problems, more debts are supposed to be made in order to save the situation. The fact that we have a system where this seems to make sense to a lot of people points out to a real problem in the setup of finance per se.

The author has followed economy and politics since the early 1970's; his main sources of information over the years have been the american "Time Magazine"; the swiss daily newspaper "Neue Zürcher Zeitung" ("NZZ"), and the british weekly magazine "The Economist".

These sources, and many other renowned publications have in the author's eye not succeeded in a satisfactory analysis of the crisis that started in 2007, none of them really went down to the roots of this crisis, none of them saw any of it coming, none of them has provided a set of measures that would solve it.

Standard theories and views as observed in many public discussions on various TV channels around the world have failed to master the subject, so the author set for himself the goal to find out what is going on and elaborate potential solutions.

He set out to read a number of books and publications that provided help, these being, in random order:

1) Debt: the first 5000 years; by David Graeber
2) Wohlstand für alle; by Ludwig Erhard
3) Griechenland - eine €uropäische Tragödie; by Wassilis Aswestopoulos
4) Wirtschaft wirklich verstehen; by Rahim Taghizadegan
5) Indignez-vous; by Stephane Hessel
6) Der Nebel um das Geld; by Bernd Senf
7) Die blinden Flecken der Oekonomie; by Bernd Senf
8) The Creature from Jekyll Island; by Edward G. Griffin
9) The Power of Gold; by Peter L. Bernstein
10) The debt-deflation theory of Great Depressions; by Irving Fisher

On top of that,
11) lecture videos that Prof. Bernd Senf has published on Youtube have been very helpful
12) the french monthly magazine "Alternatives Economiques" has proved a refreshing supplement to standard fare
13) many thanks to Wikipedia and the infinite amount of information that it freely provides
14) the website of the European Central Bank (ECB) has provided most of the numbers used later on

Based on this input, the author has mulled his own reflections and synthesis, and as a result of these deliberations offers in this document his reasoned set of opinions, and proposals, at this moment in time.
He is ready to discuss all these points, learn from others and update the script as new and/or better information and reasoning comes in.
Many of these individual points can be read in other places, but not as a full set as you may find here.
The opportunity is also taken to voice an opinion on a number of subjects that shape our lives and daily news.

The author, a Luxembourg citizen, lives in Luxembourg, in the middle of Europe, within the EuroZone of 2014, so most numbers are reflecting Europe and Euros, but the reasoning will be just as valid for other economic zones, at other times.

You can easily contact him at the email address: jcswork@pt.lu

2. *Definitions*

With the symbol € for the Euro, and in order to avoid confusion later on, let us define:

1×10^3 € =   1 000 € =   1 **Kilo** €   = 1 KE
                    (Thousand in English; mille in French; Tausend in German)

1×10^6 € =   1 000 000 € =   1 **Million** € = 1 ME
                                        (million, in all these languages)

1×10^9 € =   1 000 000 000 € =   1 **Billion** € = 1 BE
                                        (milliard in French; Milliarde in German)

1×10^{12} € =   1 000 000 000 000 € =   1 **Trillion** € = 1 TE
                                        (billion in French; Billion in German ...)

3. EURO-Zone financial situation

at the end of 2009

Geldmenge M3

In Mrd. €

NZZ chart on
Monetary Mass M3;
5-11-2011

NZZ-INFOGRAFIK/cke.

For the EuroZone,
> the following numbers do apply at the end of 2009:

			source
-	monetary mass M3 was at	~ 9,50 TE	*(NZZ; 5-11-2011)*
-	Gross Domestic Product GDP	~ 8,97 TE	*(Eurostat)*
-	total sovereign debt at	~ 7,06 TE	"
-	total government income at	~ 3,64 TE	"
-	total government budget at	~ 4,20 TE	"
-	total government deficit at	~ 0,56 TE	"

Estimating that money circulates once per month like the salary of most
of us,

- circulation or GDP per month is
> ~ 0,75 TE (= 8,97 / 12),
>   or
> ~ 7,9 %   (= 0,75 / 9,5) of M3

Impertinent Question (**I**): where is all the rest of M3 ?

It is interesting to see that

- only 7,9 % of the money is circulating at any moment in time, creating work and salaries

- sovereign debt is ~ **79 % of GDP**
  (= 7,06 / 8,97)

- sovereign debt is 1,9 x yearly government revenue
  (= 7,06 / 3,64)

- sovereign debt is ~ **74 % of M3**
  (= 7,06 / 9,5)

It seems that somehow most of M3 ends up as sovereign debt. This will need some comments later on.

Note 1: whether the EuroZone definition of M3 makes sense or not will not be discussed here. We will assume that M3 represents the amount of money in existence, however it came to exist.

Note 2: it can be seen that the M3 curve flattens out after the crisis hit at the end of 2008.

Note 3: more recent data is available at any moment in time, but does not change the points that are being made.

4. Money & debt creation

There is a saying that money governs the world - a few more impertinent questions (**II**) therefore are:

- Who governs the money?
- **How** is money governed?
  one more question here:
  Has **this** ever been a subject of public debate, or vote?

- Who ends up with the money?
- Who gets stuck with the debt?
- To whom is the debt owned?

A short look at the essence of our money and its creation will help.

The Central Bank issues money and an equal amount of debt towards banks.

The commercial bank system issues (giral-)money and an equal amount of debt towards individuals, companies, sovereigns.
It is constrained only by
- the ratio between money&debt issued to money&debt they have from central bank and from depositors
- the willingness of someone to borrow more money and get deeper in debt

In short, there is practically no money without an equal amount of debt! Small wonder that there is so much debt to go around ...

Definition: let us define **Money-Debt** (**MD**) as the pair of money&debt that are being issued by Central Bank or commercial bank

Given that interest on all that debt gets added to the debt, or has to be paid for by money from another debt, debt tends to rise faster than money.
In order to pay for that without reducing M3, more money&debt needs to be created. At any moment in time, debt grows faster that money.

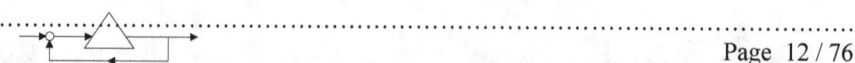

Let us introduce the concepts of

Debt   : D
Debt rate of change : DP   (mathematical derivative of D)
Total mass of debt : D3   (similar to M3)
D3 rate of change   : D3P   (mathematical derivative of D3)
M3 rate of change   : M3P   (mathematical derivative of M3)

Then we have:

$$D3 \quad > \quad M3 \quad \text{and}$$
$$D3P \quad > \quad M3P$$

during times of economic growth, while both derivatives are positive,
        debt grows faster that money,
during austerity times, when everyone wants to lower his debt,
        M3P is certainly negative as total money decreases, but
        D3P is less negative than M3P as interests on D3 keep it up, so
debt is reduced slower than money.

Small wonder that the world is awash with debt.

In short, if we all would pay back our debt, there would be no money
left, we would not be able to even pay it all back as there would be a lot
of debt left over from all the interest accumulated over time :

$$D3 \quad > \quad M3$$

Coming from the perspective that:
- it needs a certain amount of money to orient resources, facilitate
exchanges, support the continued demand for work, and the payment of
our salaries,
- it is astonishing to realize that the only way to hold money is with the
implicit knowledge that someone else has to hold the equivalent debt.

Coming from the perspective that:
- money could be reflected by real goods or investments, and vice-versa
(and that point may need debate, as real goods & properties may today
serve as loan collateral at best)
- it is astonishing to see that money is reflected by debt alone

Coming from the perspective that:
- money is also used as a way to store purchasing power for the future,
- it is astonishing to learn that:

> any savings I have is another person's debt, and
> any capital a company might have to invest
> > is reflected somewhere by a debt of equal size

with all these debts being continuously augmented by the interest!!

Seen from there, there is no net capital, but after interest only net debt. We are thus dramatically undercapitalized. In fact, we as a whole society, we are not capitalized at all!

For a capitalist system, this is quite a statement.

5. *Flow of debt*

While the flow of money is already insufficiently explored these days, preventing a better understanding of what is going on, the flow of debt is explored even less.

If I get a 10 000 E (10KE) loan from the bank, I get 10KE cash (minus a few), and 10KE debt. The money I may quickly spend, it then goes its way around the economy.

The debt is most probably stuck with me for a while, along with the interests. As I pay the principal back over time, money disappears along with debt. The interest I pay is the bank's revenue.

If I decide not to pay any principal back, only the interest, that may please the bank as long as it feels I can continue to do so, and as long as the bank can afford to roll over my debt at the end of the contract. I can even increase my debt and pay more interest.

The money is gone, the debt is mine, and I have to struggle continuously to come up with the interest, to keep the bank's confidence, and I have to hope that the bank itself sees or has no trouble when the debt needs rolling over. If the debt needs really to be repaid at the end of the contract, the amount of money that I have to pay then is probably much larger than my cash flow can afford, so either I sell some assets that I might have, or I go bankrupt.

The same goes for sovereign countries.

I might have to name collateral items in order to reassure the banker as I get the loan, so I have to hope that the value of that collateral does not go down at some future moment, or at least that the bank will not notice it, or will not mind.

If the bank notices and minds, it will want other items as new or additional collateral, from one day to the other. That might very well put me into bankruptcy as well. If my house is the collateral, and its value goes down significantly, I'm in trouble not because I can't pay the rates, but because I can't offer much else as added collateral. The bank can then kick me out of the house, and sell it. (A lot of US citizens have made that experience in the last few years)

As Woody Guthrie saw it in "Pretty Boy Floyd the Outlaw":

> yes, as through this world I've wandered
> I've seen lots of funny men,
> **some will rob you with a six-gun,**
> **and some with a fountain pen**.
>
> and as through your life you travel,
> yes, as through your life you roam,
> **you won't ever see an outlaw**
> **drive a family from their home.**

A lot of sovereigns have been busily borrowing cash, spending the money and accumulating the debt. Governments have been more profligate than their courage to collect taxes from their citizens did allow, year after year, using varying excuses.

In Europe, they helped themselves with the collateral rule that was part of the Maastricht deal, stating that their debt paper is as good as any other collateral. So a bank could buy a country's debt with the (giral-fiat) money it created itself, then put the acquired bonds to the central bank as collateral for more core money from the ECB, allowing it to lend out many times more to the private sector. Great!

Governments thus had the economy utilize more money than normal, possibly with the hope to generate more growth that way, leading to a growth in tax revenues that would pay for the next round.

Whether that could eventually be the case is another matter, (and a good subject for other papers), what has mattered is the fact that it has not been the case.
Governments kept spending more than they would get in, but the subsequent growth of activity, let alone of tax income, did not happen in the expected magnitude, if at all.

So, small wonder that governments do end up with almost all the debt.

Getting out of the debt by paying it back is just as difficult for the state as it is for myself, and has on top of that grave consequences on economic activity, for the following reasons:

Paying back has to come from the live economy, so from our salaries and revenues

That way, we have less money to spend, and less work is created as a consequence, so less salaries etc. As example, look at what is happening in Greece and Spain these days.

If sovereign (state) debt is paid back to private bondholders, the money it is reflected in stays in existence but may still disappear from economic view, in the financial cloud.
In order to come up with the money to pay back this debt, the real economy however has had to redistribute the equivalent debt to others, before. The "Black Card" ("schwarzer Peter" in German) is shifted around like a hot potato.

If debt is paid back to the bank, or to the central bank, this operation does destroy the money that the economy needs to roll along.
The money does not even end up in someone else's pocket, who could at least spend it and generate work:
It does not exist anymore!!

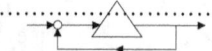

So once governments are on the slippery track of accumulating debts
that   - nobody wants to pay back while there is still time, and
        - nobody can pay back after time is up
the system is lost and ends up in a sea of debts. Witness what is going
on today.

Trying to keep the system alive despite its inherent problems, the
world's economists now separate into two camps:

- Save on the real economy to pay for the debt, thus drowning
  the real economy and its capability to pay anything (Greece)

- Keep accumulating debt to save the real economy (US)

So far from being a win-win game, the economy as we finance it today
is at best a zero-sum game, but due to the interests most probably a
negative sum game kept alive only by more debt.
This is in sharp contrast to anything I was able to read about the
economy not being a zero-sum game, in some of the world's most
renowned newspapers and magazines over the last 40 years.

Now we know where the debt ended up, and why it will stay there and
keep rising until …?

6. *Flow of IOU's (I Owe You: debt paper)*

Another question is: to whom is the debt owned?
Who are the creditors? Are they still the same ones as at the start?
If not, did they pay the same value as the initial creditor?

Here is another proposal:
If it is not the initial creditor, but someone who paid e.g. 20 % less than
its value (after discounting for maturity and interest paid), the debt
should be reduced by half the difference in value.

To make it simpler, imagine
- 100 Euro debt with no interest,
- the IOU is sold a few years after issue 20 % cheaper than the initial value, so at 80 Euro.
- the debt to be serviced should then be reduced to 90 Euro, and not stay at the top.
This would help the debtor as well.
It gets a bit more complex when interest comes in; we leave that calculation to another paper.

7. Flow of money

A few more numbers covering the trend in the years before 2009, from the same sources as mentioned on page 1:

Δ M3 /year   0,70 TE
Δ GDP/year   - 0,18 TE   (~2% growth, or 25,7 % of Δ M3)
Loss /year =   0,52 TE   lost from the economic cycle

while the public debt increases at the rate of

Δ debt/year =   0,645 TE

In the effort to support the economy,
the system adds 0,7 TE of money&debt each year (Δ M3);
but the losses of the economy are such (0,52 TE)
that only (0,70 – 0,52 =) 0,18 net are circling in the economy.

And they do that only once, not 12 times which would be at the rhythm of once per month…

So while the cash goes wherever it goes, the debt is stuck with sovereigns, its population and taxpayers, who see
        only a quarter   (0,18 / 0,70 = 0,25) of the extra cash,
            once, before it disappears altogether from view, but
        just about all of it   (0,654 / 0,70 = 0,937) => 93,7 %
            ending up as their debt!

Or rather, who are losing cash on such a grand scale that the extra money&debt is barely able to compensate for, but are accumulating debt on a 1:1 scale. Instead of seeing most of the extra money circulating around, generating work, salaries, taxes, we barely see the cash but see the full number increasing our debt.

Looking at myself and many other people, we are normally very good at paying taxes and spending our salaries on a month by month basis.

On the other hand, if I start to save 10 % of my income, and everybody does the same, we are saving 10 % of GDP that is 0,9 TE / year, more than the extra M3. If we do that every year, there will be mountain of cash after a while, reflected in a mountain of debt that we have as taxpayers.
The richer I am, the more of my income I can save to the detriment of the real economy.
The only way the money finds its way back is as debt for someone else, when the bank where I have my savings account has lent out some of it, almost all of it, or 10 times more than it…
But that will only work as long as the debtors are doing well. As soon as many debtors are in trouble, all of us are in trouble, along with banks, governments and so on.
We may all have to look at the mirror to find more culprits.

If saving is encouraged by tax breaks, like all the pension funds, this process is enhanced even more, without the freedom to spend the money as we want. In this case, the tax exemption is granted to the western baby-boomer generation that desperately wants to avoid facing the fact that the demographic pyramid wants to stand on its head.
This tax exemption is counterproductive, in the way that it encourages taking cash out of the real economy, continuously reduces the amount of work & jobs that are in demand - while piling up savings for some and debt for all.
The baby-boomer generation did put itself out of full employment that way, and the generation after us will have to service the debt at the same time as they will have to care for us…

As a baby-boomer myself, I could say "après nous le deluge", but that would be wrong (not only for moral reasons). We will not be gone yet,

and will have to witness the effects of our decisions at a moment in time when we cannot do anything about it anymore.

We will still see our children struggle through the mess we created.

8. To whose benefit?

The benefit is not to the next generation, as they are stuck with both debt and us.

The benefit is not to the baby-boomer generation, as it has deliberately put out of job a large percentage of their own, and of their children (but they may have been duped into believing it was in their best interest).

The benefit is not to the sovereign states, as they collect only debt.

The benefit is to

political systems, as they are voted back as long as they keep taxes low and spending high,

the finance industry, which got all this cash to play with, enjoying the only taxless transaction system in the world ...

Interestingly, the finance industry does not miss an opportunity to declare that we should stop paying simultaneous (pay-as-you-go) pension systems, but save and give the money to them, so that they can work or rather have fun with it. And politics does support all that with tax rebates.

As a matter of fact, the political discourse has been hijacked by the interests of tax non-payers, and the finance industry that serves them.

To go further, the finance industry wants to increase its part of the pension sector by obstructing the pay-as-you-go system, a reliable system that serves the population well, but does not contribute to the finance sector's well-being.

Riester-Rente in Germany is a good example for this desire to increase the non-simultaneous part of the pension sector.

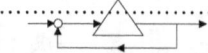

9. *Real & Cloud economy*

The economic system seems to have evolved into two parts:
- the real economy where transactions pay for products & services (thus actual work), and get taxed
- finance cloud economy, which thanks to high margins in and interests from the real economy,
    draws resources from the real economy,
    keeps resources away from it, and
    keeps them rotating untaxed around the financial world.

In order to make up for the loss of money from the real economy towards the finance cloud, governments feel obliged to borrow heavily, from the finance cloud.
The impact of the borrowed money onto the real economy is small as it disappears quickly back into the cloud, owned by people who enjoy high margins to get it, then do not want to spend it, nor risk it in real investments.

But as long as the debt is bearable, both citizens and cloud get along with it, and politicians get reelected.
Now, as both cloud and public realize that the public is in trouble, now that the public has accumulated more debt than the real economy can ever pay back, nobody finds a way out anymore.

10. Maastricht criteria : Eurozone stability & growth pact

In Maastricht, EU leaders seem to have willfully designed an unsustainable system, relying on goodwill about the european concept to wave it through.

Instead of asking for balanced public accounts,
they allowed 3% deficit/GDP; and 60% debt/GDP.

I suspect that the growth part of the pact should have come from sovereign debtmaking, hoping that there would be enough growth in the year to come so that the new debt level would not be a problem with respect to the new GDP.

Why they took GDP as denominator is hard to guess, I suspect that they took the biggest number available to make deficit & debt look smaller.

A more reasonable number would have been state income, or at least state real budget level.

Typically, with a 40% target government share of an economy, GDP is 2,5 times bigger than the state turnover,

so a deficit ratio of 3% to GDP is 3 x 2,5 = 7,5 % on government turnover.

A debt ratio of 60% with respect to GDP transforms into 60 x 2,5 = 150 % , with respect to government turnover!

Imagine yourself spending each year 7,5 % more than you earn, and relying on next year's pay raise to care for that. So what happens when there is no pay raise for a while, or worse: when your company is not doing well and you lose your job.

So this is what happens now:

in a recession, GDP recedes, making the denominator smaller, tax income recedes even faster, increasing the deficit nominator, and the ratio deficit/GDP rises fast.

Trying to get back to the intended ratio by increasing the tax rate on the still existing part of the economy will depress that too; reduce tax income even more, starting a vicious circle downhill.

If at least we could all agree on keeping the budget stable in nominal terms, for several years, until economy and tax income have recuperated and debt can be paid back. That way, there would be no vicious circle, and the state would work as a damper in this dynamic system.

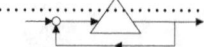

The only spending rise should be to pay for the rising unemployment.

Tax increases should hit the financial cloud and its tributaries, not the real economy where money circulates while generating work.

Since the extra cash from the growth pact was funneled into the economy through the state and therefore oriented according to political criteria, it typically did not generate much growth, just added to the debt.

This process flourished for a while, until it became clear to everyone that it is unsustainable. By now, it is too late for everybody.

Maastricht and later amendments have foreseen penalties for exceeding the limits decided on, but the penalties are financial, so can make matters only worse. This penalty concept is an illusion and can never be applied.

The discipline that we were all expecting from the EuroZone organization was not confirmed. While the Germans had been the one's insisting on the stability part of the contract, they were the first to break it themselves after a few years. The French then did the same. Everybody else was watching and drawing their conclusions.

11. Central Banking

There is another point that keeps haunting me in these respects:
A large part of a government's debt papers are auctioned off publicly by the treasury, to whoever demands the lowest interest.
Some of them are bought by private persons or institutions, some of them by commercial banks, and depending on the economic zone, some by the Central Bank.
In the UK, the central bank is the Bank of England, and in that system the role of the debt papers bought by the central bank is quite interesting, as the whole system is based on public debt owed to the Central Bank.
Here a simplified, 3-step explanation of UK money creation:

The **Bank of England (BoE)**

1 :   **buys** government **debt** "X", pays "X" to the treasury,
and asks for interest

based on that public **debt**
2 :   **creates** public debt notes (for the same amount "X"),
which are money: pound sterling
these (paper or virtual) notes can be borrowed by the
commercial banks (for interest),
and are counted by those as "**reserves**"

based on those **reserves**, and on the requirement for minimum fractional reserve ratios (say 5 or 10 % of loan total to be held as reserves)
3:   **allows** the commercial banks to
create 10 or 20 times more "**money**" than "X" ,
when lending out against interest, (1/0.10 or 1/0.05)
and of course to
issue the same amount of new **debt**

This process allows quick increases of money&debt supply into the economy, but is based on the UK state going further into debt, and on private companies and citizens to be in the mood for borrowing more.

It also means that the state better not start to repay the debt it owes the Central Bank, as each pound paid back to the Bank of England would require 10 or 20 times more money to be pulled out of the economy by the commercial banks, who in order to respect their factional reserve requirements, would be obliged to reduce their loan book accordingly.

There is also the part of public debt that is bought by private persons, institutions from home or from abroad.
These are being paid by existing money, which had been created during some earlier loop.
Then there is the part of the public debt bought directly by commercial banks:
These bonds are also allowed to serve as reserves for further lending, as described before.

The process is quite smooth as long as things go "well", that means public debt goes up, Bank of England debt note creation goes up, commercial bank purchasing of government bonds goes up, private borrowing at commercial banks goes up even faster, and interests are being paid by the private companies and citizens because these are all doing better as the economy does better.

As long as the sun is shining, nobody minds the fact that everybody gets deeper in debt, and that everybody pays his dues in terms of interests, not to be confused with taxes.

Things get more interesting when the mood changes, when the economy sputters, when a number of debts cannot be served anymore, when some borrowers start to get late on the interest payments, when people or companies have misdirected their investments, when citizens are tight on paying off their consumer loans. when the private sector stops wanting to borrow some more and instead wants to reduce its load of debt.

In that case, by way of the fractional reserve requirements, any reduction of the sovereign debt causes a much faster reduction of the money supply and circulation, leading to immediate deflation and depression. For that reason, within the current system, the UK could not

even get out of debt anymore, even if the citizens and government all wanted to get out. The US is in the same situation, for the same reasons. So the best we can hope for is to stabilize the debt at some level.

These public debts weigh on all citizens and taxpayers, the interest is paid by all. But the benefit of the interest does not go to all, only to those who own the debt papers. Some of them are held by the central bank, so we can consider that to be a representation of the citizenship as well.

But much of them are held by private citizens, institutions, banks, foreigners. And these will benefit from the interest payments, as long as the state can afford to pay them out of our taxes, or out of the inflation we may be asked to tolerate.

Looking at our deposits at the local bank, we have to see that the wondrous multiplication of money through fractional reserve banking is also applied to these deposits, and if more of us are pulling out our money from that bank, the bank will be first in trouble because it has to pay us back with paper cash or computer money, but next it will be seriously in trouble as the fractional reserve requirements demand an

a) increase of reserves, and/or an
b) appropriate reduction on the loan book.

So what might happen ?

a) If there is no increase of reserves by a set of bank shareholders, or some more credit from the Central Bank, it may have to close the door.
b) No more new credit to anyone, decrease the amount of outstanding loans whenever possible, thus destroying money and reduce overall circulation thereof.

If that happens in more places than one, we have a crisis, recession, severe recession, depression, misery, war ?
Such is the lack of stability of our monetary system.

Today, I wonder whether our EuroZone public debt does also serve the purpose of increasing money supply, just like in the UK or the US.

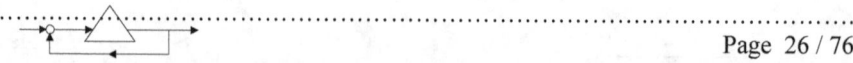

The EuroZone has allowed its commercial banks to count public debt from any of its members as reserves, as basis for fractional reserve lending.

I did not read any of that in the European Constitution that we voted on in 2005, at least in Luxembourg and a few other countries.

Could we have a large discussion on the aspects of how money should be governed, including this point!?

All was OK as long as all was OK, things stopped being OK when the financial crisis (2008) revealed the poor quality of many investments made, by both private and public in many countries.

A lot of private lenders then realized that some of those countries might not be able to pay their interest, and therefore the lenders would not roll over their debt any longer. That was the start of the public debt crisis.

12. Maastricht revisited : Proposals I

The stability & growth pact as well as the Maastricht criteria need to change as follows:

- evaluate deficits and debt as a function of last year's state income
- keep last year's budget total stable for this year
- if there is more tax money coming in, repay your debt
- if your debt is repaid, and more money comes in, increase next year's budget by the differential amount
- **growth money needs to come from central bank, distributed to each citizen, as money-no-debt (MND)**
- unsustainable balance of payment divergences to be handled via exchange rates
- Government to be financed by taxes, not by debt
- everyone to pay taxes, every company as well, and every transaction including financial one's
- care has to be taken that "enough" money stays in the real economy
- **the target size of cloud / savings economy needs to be discussed, as well as its rules**

subsequently,
- **care has to be taken that newly generated money-no-debt (MND) can also compensate for losses to the cloud economy and savings**

This last point will take most of the interest issue out of the system, on a continuous basis.

13. Market economy

We all like to go to the market and buy the best vegetables for the cheapest price, and enjoy the fact that vendors compete hard on margins and cost.

In our job, we typically do enjoy it much less when a competitor comes up selling something very similar, or better, at a lower price.

This reduces our income.

So the effort goes into creating a monopoly situation for the things that I sell, while enjoying a real market situation for the things that I buy.

This can be called asymmetric behavior: destroy my competitor, but call for more competition in the supermarket.

If I am successful in both, I get rich.

Observing closed markets for a while, it becomes clear that after a while, there are only a few players left: very often a leader who sets the pace, a follower, and a scrambling survivor (like GM, Ford, and Chrysler in the US before the Japanese came in)

So left to itself, market conditions will favor the rise of huge market shares for a few, who try to dominate and eliminate the market situation.

After a longer while, there is only one left, and we have a real monopoly, the monopolist getting really rich.

If it hadn't been for anti-trust concerns, GM would have flattened the other two, to stand alone after that.

So, while we all appreciate market economy in the supermarket and try to avoid it at our job, keeping market conditions alive is the challenge for the framework provider that is the state. The later it gets down to this job, the harder it gets as the very interests that need to be stopped are increasing their financial and political power all the time. Better bust the trust in the early stages.

Teddy Roosevelt managed to bust the powerful monopolies of his time (like Rockefeller's Standard Oil), and deserves our respect for that.

Conclusion: The Market economy is fine, but you can't leave it alone for too long. The framework provider needs to keep all the participants in check.

14. Social market economy

Who should get which part of the benefit from the efforts: customer; company, personnel, management, shareholders, debtholders, stakeholders?

Again, if you leave it all to market forces, results become ugly over time, depending on which of these "partners" achieves a monopolistic situation and wants to use it.

Careful balancing needs to take place in order to avoid problems. This is a task for decent management, not for shareholders.

If nobody cares for the company, investments will not be made, equipment will age, products will become obsolete, the company will become obsolete.

If all the benefits go to the customer, misery will loom for all others, and they will stop the show if they can afford it.

If it all goes to personnel as cash and/or workplace, shareholders & debtholders will be concerned, the workforce may or may not get complacent.

If it all goes to shareholders, then to debtholders, with management kept quiet by their bribes, personnel will feel cheated, and customers will soon suffer from lack of innovation, quality, service, and high cost.

This last effect is what we are seeing these days with all the private equity leveraged buy-outs, and the emphasis on shareholder value.

If stakeholders, like local communities, do not benefit from the activity, but even suffer from environmental drawbacks, they will be glad when you leave.

Looking back at what Ludwig Erhard has done in Germany a few years after WW II, it is clear that if employment and decent living conditions are a goal of a society, a good part of the benefit of work and progress needs to end up
>   with customers and personnel,
>   who make money go round and thereby create work,
>   rather than with a cloud, where it just sits or circulates around
>   without facilitating any value-added work,
>   and is lacking in the real economy.

The part of the benefit that stays with the company can be reinvested into new capacities & capabilities, the part getting towards shareholders is better kept within a reasonable (0 .. 5 % after inflation) relationship with the real & current value of the equity once put in.

Hot air, like extensive "goodwill" after a buy-up, should not appear on the accounts of the company, neither on the left side (as goodwill) nor on the right side (as debt). If debt is protracted to buy the company, debt should be with the buyer, not the company.

The overall amount of circulating money going into savings has to be watched by the Central Bank and the finance minister, as it is pulled out of the circuit, destroys activity and generates unemployment.
It needs to be compensated by fresh money from the central bank, issued not as money-debt, but as money-no-debt (MND) to avoid further problems. This will over time generate an overhang of saved money, but at least not of the debt that today goes with it.
This overhang today is more than 10 times larger than the money that is allowed to circulate, thus hanging like a Damocles sword over efforts to facilitate stable economies with sustainable growth.
It is currently used to intentionally or unintentionally cause short term unbalances in the real economy, which cannot react fast enough to avoid misery in the areas concerned.
Most areas do welcome an income of outside/saved money, as it allows job creation, infrastructure build-up and so on.
But, pull the money out or even stop putting in some more and crisis looms in areas concerned, which have no time to adjust their real economy to the sudden downward change.

The Asian Crisis in the late 90's was a testimony to that. This leads to the conclusion that large overhanging savings are fine as they represent our well-being and fortune, but the manner with which it can be pushed into and pulled out of any real economy needs to be managed locally, by the local institutions. Sticky investments are then a must. Capital controls of some kind will have to come back.
Forget about unbridled movement of capital. It is just too dangerous!

15. *Financial Industry reshaped : Proposals II*

The (real-existierender) business model of commercial banks has forfeited its credibility for good by mid 2012, as most of them had to be saved by their governments, or the ECB, once or twice.

Today they
>   are stuck with bad debts from public & private,
>   are under pressure to raise their equity to fulfill
>   Basel III criteria and
>   are therefore unwilling to lend out any money to the
>   real economy, depriving it of capital badly needed.

Their effort to save money to add to their equity means that rather than putting badly needed money into the real economy, they subtract money from it and generate even more misery. The money to shore up the banks had better come from the overhanging cloud.

Since it does not seem to do so, the question is: who needs such institutions?

My proposal is to create a robust set of institutions whose dealings are understandable to everyone, and whose participants have no inherent conflicts of interest.

Proposal: the money we save goes to

-    The **Financial Service Institution (I)**, a **central savings** and **transaction** institution,

which may or may not give us interest to compensate for inflation, but not more. But it guarantees the savings in the name of the country, or in our case, Europe. It does nothing with the money, does not invest it anywhere, does not speculate, does not lend. It just manages the flow of money between actors. Everybody has a couple of accounts at this institution, one for the savings, and one for the daily operations. It is the clearing system for all, and it has to be managed and controlled in a professional manner.

Many postal banking systems around the world operate partly in similar ways, for instance my luxemburgish postal check account manages my transactions well and efficiently, and this system had done just as well for my parents and grand-parents.

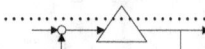

If today I want interest (more than inflation), I put my money to a commercial bank, which will help me invest it wisely (?), or lends out to borrowers.

My proposal is to separate investment and lending/borrowing, give the first to the fund industry, and the second to:

-   Financial Service Industry (**II**): the **new banking industry**

The **new bank** is a private company; its shareholders put in their own money, which is at risk, and get the other money they need from the central bank at the prevailing interest rate. There needs to be a healthy relationship between money lent out and its risk, and equity invested by the bank's shareholders. My proposal would be **33 % equity** as reserve, so the bank would be allowed to lend three times more money than its shareholders have put in. The actual ratios are set by the central bank and should not change too quickly, so that the new bank or the real economy is not jeopardized.

The bank does not receive money from savers, so they do not put it at risk.

The bank does not pay out any cash, but credits the borrowers' account at the central savings institute. So no bank raid, no run on a bank.

The bank does not create (giral-)money/debt on its own, but borrows any needed money from the central bank. Thus, the central bank knows at any moment in time what the financial situation of the bank is. Within the limits given by the equity/lending ratio, the new bank is free to lend as it wants, but must keep the central bank informed about the direction of its lending, and the central bank may offer some non-binding comments. This may avoid too much money flowing into the same sector.

Private persons will not have the classical deposits at the bank, so those deposits will not be at risk.

If they want to put money back into circulation, by investing it within banks, they can apply for being shareholders of the bank, which may stabilize or increase its balance sheet that way. Shareholders get dividends if things go well, none if things do not go well, and their capital is at risk when things turn sour. No bailing out from others, certainly not from the state.

Banks will not grow to be "too big to fail". Anything private that is "too big to fail" is just too big, and has to be broken up before it generates problems.

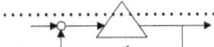

-   The Financial Service Industry (**III**) will be available to set up the **sale of shares and bonds**, and the **trade** thereof. It will not trade itself in those shares & bonds, but ensure the quality of information around them, and easy access to its services for everyone. A set of transaction taxes will be defined, and FS-III will pay them directly to the state treasury at the time of the transaction.

-   The Financial Service Industry (**IV**) will **advise investors** big & small as to how to manage their wealth, for a fee.

-   The Financial Service Industry (**V**) will **set up and manage funds**. Fund managers are independent and have no stakes themselves in the companies they deal with.
Fund managers make sure that taxes get paid on earnings.
Any takeover will require at least 51% of capital in "cash", not borrowed from a bank.
Any takeover will prohibit putting debt contracted for the takeover onto the balance sheet of the company.
The buyer has to live with the maximum dividend the company can pay without putting the company's own well-being at risk. Management will be selected and supervised by the board that includes representatives of stakeholders and personnel.
The investor himself knowingly puts his money at risk, via shares, funds, bonds; he reaps the rewards of success and of failure. No bail-out from the state.

The investor will pull his money from his central savings account to the investment vehicle, incurring transaction tax as defined.
No tax rebates for investment.
With a nod to Islamic Banking, interests paid on bonds will not be fixed but will remain subject to business success, and bonds will all or partly by converted to equity if the debt proves unmanageable.

-   The Financial Service Industry (**VI**) will be the **insurance industry**, not connected to the other services. It will concentrate on covering risk, and sell neither declared nor hidden pension plans.

There will be no mix between the different levels of financial service industry, no one-stop company (bank) who does it all and therefore gets into conflicts of interest. Problems from one area will not flow towards the others, since there will be no other areas under the same umbrella.

In short, here is the proposed future

Financial Service Industry (FSI):

I. save money : central savings & transaction institution
(collecting all savings, making all transactions, paying no real interest)

II. lend money: new bank industry
(no giral-money creation, no cash)

III. set up the sale of shares and bonds
(organize IPO's & bond emissions, then facilitate trade thereof)

IV. advise investors
(only advice, no self-invest)

V. set up and manage funds
(manage only other people's money !)

VI. insurance industry
(neither pension nor social security, only material risk)

All independent from each other!

Definition: **IPO** = Initial Public **O**ffering;
or the first emission of shares by a company

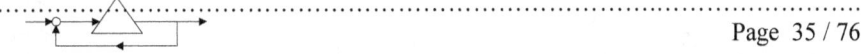

16. Pensions

The baby-boomer scare of ending their life within an upside-down age pyramid, and its effect on pension systems and real economy has already be mentioned, it needs to be addressed.

Pension will be paid by simultaneous contributions within the real economy, with limited reserves to avoid a negative impact on the economy, and prevent speculation with the funds.

If needed it will be supplemented by a pension tax on all savings in the central savings bank, or by taxes on the real economy.

Individual pension rights are derived from individual pay-ins during activity time, and the relation to past & current GDP, and current pay-in levels.

All attempts to pull the linen closer to ourselves (as we get old) will fail as there are not more people actually working anyway.

Investing in foreign countries with a younger population may be an option, as people in these countries might readily pay for us when we are old, having benefited from our money while we still had some. Whether they really will do that remains to be seen, decades later…

It also might be necessary to invest in that foreign country's education and economic infrastructure before seeing any benefit come back.

Contributions should be linear with personal income, without an upper limit, as they should end up being proportional to GDP.

17. Social Security

Will also be based on pay-as-you-go, with limited reserves to avoid a negative impact on the economy, and prevent speculation.

It will be covering risks like illness, invalidity or early death. It will also actively pursue prevention, in medical, health, safety and other fields.

There should be one obligatory system - and only one - per country or region, and efforts should be made to manage this very well, using benchmarking to make individual systems progress.

Supplementary plans can coexist for wealthier people who want new and expensive treatments, but the basic system has to offer effective lifetime-efficient services to all. These services may get expanded over time as new research & development (R&D) results come in, as the cost of new treatments comes down and their effectiveness goes up.

Again, contributions should be linear with personal income, without an upper limit, as they should end up being proportional to GDP.

18. Public versus Private Debt

For a closed economy, a well-known formula in economics is:

$$(S - I) + (T - G) = 0 \qquad \text{or} \qquad PS + GS = 0 \quad PS = - GS$$

S : private Savings
I : private Investment
T : Tax income
G : Government spending

PS : Private Surplus	$PS = (S - I)$
GS : Government Surplus	$GS = (T - G)$

So, any government surplus is the private sector's minus, and vice-versa. If the government makes no debt, the private sector will not make surplus!! In the current system, the private sector can only get richer, if the public gets poor!!

To keep things sustainable means to keep both close to zero, or fluctuating not far from it.

For the community as a whole, it makes no sense running up private surpluses, as it means running up governmental debts at the same rate.

Government should therefore have an adequate tax and spend rate, to keep it all at equilibrium.

Things get a bit more complex if the world outside our economy puts and pulls money in and out:

$$(S - I) + (T - G) = (X - M) \qquad \text{or} \qquad PS + GS = DXM$$
$$\text{with} \quad DXM = (X - M)$$

with
X : inflow of money = value of exports + profits of home companies abroad + inflows or transfers through banks

M : outflow of money= costs of imports + profits of foreign companies in our country + outflows or transfers through banks

DXM : balance of accounts

- If there is a net inflow of cash from outside, it will go to either private or public pockets, or towards both.
- If there is an outflow of cash to the outside world, it has to come from either private or public coffers, or from both.

A sustainable system will balance this well between private & public, and will also aim at reducing the imbalance of accounts itself.

- If DXM stays negative, and private finances are unchanged, the state will eventually go bankrupt, while some of its citizens are still rich.
- If DXM stays negative for a long time and the pain is balanced, both public and private will end up bankrupt.

They therefore have an interest in improving things, together.

- If DXM is positive and public finances do not profit, some of its citizens get very rich. If at the same time the state's finances may deteriorate anyway, the state may go bankrupt despite the good business its citizens have, despite some of those citizens getting richer.

That is the case in Germany today, where after years of huge trade surpluses, and public debt increasing anyway, one can only conclude that the state has been stupid enough to let that happen, or has been dominated by decision-makers

with their own interest in letting it happen, or
with the aim of pleasing their part of the electorate.

Let us inject some central bank money-no-debt (MND) to the equation:

$$(S - I) + (T - G) = (X - M) + MND$$

We could imagine that in order to reflect the real things that we built, the services we have delivered over the year, the increased (at least nominal) GDP that we have generated, or that we should generate, should be reflected by an increase in our own money supply.
Or that by political decision we think it appropriate that we can save x % of our income for a rainy day or for some bigger expense later on.

That could easily be done by having the central bank generate that x % of GDP as money-no-debt. In order to treat everyone equally, each person within the central bank's authority should have the same amount, or at least an amount reflecting his/her country's GDP.

So let us keep public finances as well as trade & current accounts balanced, and build up private savings with the help of the Central Bank.

That will certainly not lead to the same savings for each, but it will open the door to savings that do not imply debt for someone else.

Another observable option is:

Central Bank prints money-no-debt MND and gives it to the government to plug budget holes, and just those :

$(S - I) + (T + \mathbf{MND} - G) = (X - M)$

$MND = G - T$ (new money = spending minus tax income)

$\Rightarrow (T + MND - G) = 0$

The private net result will then be equal to balance of payments

$(S - I) = (X - M)$

Or: The Central Bank wants interest ($\mathbf{II}$) for that

$(S - I) + (T + MND - G - \mathbf{II}) = (X - M)$

Or: private folks & institutions lend their surplus cash from last year (**PLC**, Private Lending Cash) to the government to plug budget holes, for interest

$(S - I) + (T + \mathbf{PLC} - G - \mathbf{II}) = (X - M)$

or worse: foreign folks lend (**FLC**, Foreign Lending Cash) to the government to plug budget holes, for interest

$(S - I) + (T + \mathbf{FLC} - G - \mathbf{II}) = (X - M)$

On the last 3 scenarios, things go sour at the latest when freshly borrowed money needed to plug holes is just enough to pay the interest.

That day, expenses are on the same level as tax income, where they should have been all along, with the interesting difference that the country is deeply in debt by now. The day after, interest rates may rise, and now expenses need to go down at last, damaging the economy.

   II >= PLC   : with lenders that live in the country, the government could still find an arrangement with its citizens

   II >= FLC : with foreign lenders, government goes bankrupt

It gets even worse when lenders refuse to renew and roll over the loans, loans then need to be paid back right away, not only their interest. Now that will really hurt the real economy, from which now also the principal, formerly circulating money, is subtracted, leaving less to circulate and create activity.

This is what has happened, in Europe, at least before the European Central Bank stated that it will save the Euro by whatever means.

If only the former lenders would then spend the cash that they get back as principal, that would at least revive the economy!

If only we would spend our money instead of saving 10... 15 % of our income.

If only we would stop accumulating private savings while knowing (or maybe not) that someone else will be stuck with the equivalent debt, and other persons with the equivalent lack of jobs.

Can we tell people not to save? Isn't that going against a very basic human trait?

How to acknowledge our desire for saving, and still do something to maintain our jobs?

Well, I do not like the concept of governments drowning in debt just to make some of us rich. The solution is not for the government to spend less, but to spend the same and raise taxes in order to balance the running accounts. It has to raise taxes smartly, so that only the cash that would otherwise disappear into the clouds gets caught.

If it doesn't achieve that over time, my suspicion is that interest groups are preventing that to happen, through lobbying. They must be check-mated!

The same cash that would be lent to the government, it has to take in as tax, before!

On the other hand, the overall tax rate should not exceed a reasonable number, a number that should be agreed to by the community (40 %?). Having it too big will kill economic activity, having it too small will make differences in lifestyles too large.
But whatever the ratio is, the accounts must be balanced.

Do not get into arguments like that savers need government bonds to invest in, savers should put their money into the central savings account. If they want more return, they have to take more risk, and invest in economic activities, in real companies. I would not allow them to feel entitled to me paying their interest just because the tax rate is too low. That doesn't go!

At the end of 2012, the US was looking forward to what they called the "fiscal cliff", where there should be simultaneously a 5 % tax hike, and a 5% reduction in government outlays. It came to that because the two parties in Congress could not agree on how to run the federal finances. But they still avoided the worst between Election Day and fiscal-cliff-day.
The author's comment is that the tax hike is fine as long as it hits the money that would otherwise disappear in the cloud, and not the real economy.
The reduction in overall outlays is counterproductive as it reduces the real economy by the same percentage, thus causing more recession.
The goal is to keep the real economy at current level by whatever means, even unconventional one's, and let the economy go further as soon as it stands on its own feet again.
Reducing the real economy will stage a vicious circle, where nothing will be achieved except widespread misery.

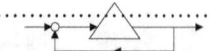

19. Wealth

We all would like to get or be rich, being rich meaning having a lot more discretionary money and property than most of the others.

Most of us are not very rich, but all of us would like to hold on to what we have, and certainly hold on to the value of the money that we hold.

We all know that shares can go up and down, dividends may get paid or not, our enterprises may succeed or go under.

But we do not like the thought of our cash savings getting eroded by inflation, or erased by the failure of our bank. We also do not appreciate being told that for the sake of the real economy and of money circulation we should not save so much.

My proposal is therefore to put our savings into a national central savings institution, as described in the chapter on the reshaping of the financial industry. This institution does not lend out any of our money, but pays interest to compensate for inflation, not more. Anyone who wants to get richer by having his money "work" should contact the other actors of the new finance industry.

Anyone who wants to hold on to what he has, stays with the savings account, guaranteed by the state, with inflation off-setting interest generated as money-no-debt by the central bank. There should be no limit on the amounts allowed, but the citizens allowed in have to be living within the community covered by the central bank, the government, and the statistics office that calculates the inflation rate.

In times of crisis, recessions, deficits, that wealth can also be taxed, rather than mobilized by bonds.

We can also imagine periods of paying less interest than the inflation rate, say 50 % of that.

If monetary wealth has been spent to buy property, at least it does not hold back money from circulation anymore. Whether and how that property, or its proceeds, has to be taxed is less a question of monetary stability than of social "justice", and should not be treated here.

We should also recognize that the real wealth the society has is its capability to generate it, or to regenerate it if needed.

So what makes us rich is the things we know, and the way we get organized at putting them to good use, and then to work at it.

So, education, functional organization (politics, companies), and hard work are important whatever cash we have or might not have.

20. The problem today

In the EuroZone, the situation has been deteriorating for more than 10 years, since right from the start. "Investors" did lend money to efficient countries at the same rates as to non-efficient one's, with the result that the latter got much more than they should normally get, at low rates.

Now these non-efficient countries have spent the money, in poor investments or for downright consumer goods, they are stuck with the debt they never wanted to pay back, and rates go up.

The damage is done. It cannot be reversed since the real economy in those places cannot keep itself up and running, let alone deliver enough money to pay for the interest, not even thinking about the principal.

In the same countries, banks have got money from the central bank at the same rates as efficient countries, and have gone quite wild by lending self-produced (giral/fiat-)money to private and public alike. So not only public debt is unserviceable, but there is a lot of private debt that is in trouble as the economy is stuck.

The situation now is quite desperate, with former bondholders not wanting to roll over their sovereign bonds, and real countries facing real depression or outright bankruptcy, most of their banks as well, and many of their citizens too. That does not bode well for the political stability of our economic zone.

A crisis of this kind has in the past often led to strange figures coming into power, and war. (see the great depression of the 30', its effect on Germany, and World War II after that)

So alternative thinking, and acting, is the order of the day.

It is evident that no country will be able to pay back its debt anytime soon, that unless we act, some will be first to go bankrupt and towards civil strife, some will come right after, the rest will follow suit.

The money is gone, debtors have had an economic boom (at least some of them), and bankers have had a party. Both boom and party are now over, although the author is not yet sure about the party at the banks.

Creditors have been stupid and do not really deserve our sympathies, neither for the fact that they did avoid taxes so well in the first place, nor for the fact that they did not want to spend their money themselves and recreate economic activity, nor for the fact that they lent out their money recklessly.

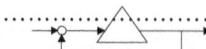

What also has happened since we started the Euro, and what was amazingly well described and warned against by Prof. Bernd Senf on the last pages of his book (" Der Nebel um das Geld"), notabene in 1996, well before we introduced the Euro, is that stronger, more cohesive and disciplined countries would gain significant market shares at the expense of the others, and would not be penalized by reevaluation of their currency as we all have the same Euro.

And the weaker countries could not help themselves by devaluation, where the nominal cost base within the country would stay the same, but the real cost base of the whole country would come down. They would have had to politically muster the will to reduce their real cost by reducing their nominal cost base, so their salaries, rents, mortgages, debts etc, and do it without putting their economy into a downward spiral. These things can only work, if at all, in countries with little public or private debt, but not where lots of debt is around that can quickly turn sour.

Or they would need to elevate their productivity and innovative performance to match their cost base. That would be the optimal solution, requiring the political will to make the necessary structural changes in order to stay competitive, or get there again.

But none of this has happened.

What happened instead under the watchful eye of local and european politicians was the following:

Faced with about 5 million people unemployed, budget deficits, and an unwillingness of their richer citizens to spend their cash, Germany had to do something in the early 2000's.

They had roughly the choice of either

a) getting their richer citizens to pay more tax
- rather than buy more bonds, or
- rather than hide their cash away in tax-avoidance countries

or

b) lowering labor cost (by stabilizing it over time)
- to make the whole economy more competitive when compared to outside,

and
- continue watching their successful exporters big and small buying german bonds or accumulating their cash in tax heavens

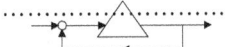

The outside world has no vote in Germany, and in principle has only itself to blame if it can't get more competitive.

Unemployment in Germany dutifully came down towards 3 million and below, export business picked up, german business prospered as did the balance of trade with huge surpluses reflecting the performance and competitiveness of the german society.

Unfortunately, public deficits also continued to prosper; infrastructure, communities, schools did not.

So as Germany kept its cost level stable within the agenda 2010 effort, it got more competitive by the year and german companies big and small made a lot of money. Their owners used big portions of that money also to buy the sovereign bonds that allowed the weaker countries to live well for a while and to avoid needed structural changes. They were not the only one's putting their money into those bonds.

Now the southern economies are in shambles, the structures that would have needed those changes are destroyed and hardly revivable, the debts are there and cannot be serviced, devaluation cannot happen, deflation is the order of the day, and depression looms around the corner.

It is doubtful whether these economies can be revived any time soon, as their people's competences may not be useful anymore after their factory (or office) has shut down.

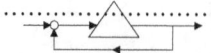

21. Germany's (the ?) problem

All in all, without really wanting such a result, and while still having difficulties grasping the result, and based only upon its work ethics, Germany now has won the last round of european wars. This round has been an economic one. Let us at least keep it that way.
It has been costly for Germany as well.

But what do you do when you have won a war? Especially when you are also deeply indebted !?
Get the others to work for you, pay your rent, pay your pension? After having de facto destroyed their working base?
What do you do when you (wrongly) think that the (BundesBank-)system that governs (y)our money is superior, although what really is superior is the performance of your engineers and workers, and your governance of everything, except of money?

You had been able to start anew with no debts after Ludwig Erhard's Währungsreform, so the debt/interest issue has not been a problem during the first generation after that. Now, after the second generation, debt build-up becomes more than apparent, and doom looms over the monetary system and Bundesbank mentality. See german public debt levels!
But now you see a chance of extending the duration of the system by doing (exporting) more of the same, flattening every one else on the way?
What is the purpose of such proceedings? Live better and happier after breaking the back of your neighbors? Revenge for lost wars?

My advice would be to use your money to make real investments, allowing people to work. If you want to benefit from a war won, you at least have to offer the others a way to make their living, and thus being able to pay "reparation", or "tribute". If that is what you want.

And you should not overstretch the Versailles bow! Please avoid playing a Clemenceau! Don't get the old train wagon back to Compiègne!

22. The way out: immediate action : Proposals III

The only way out now is for the central bank to buy the debt. All of it. As the bonds come due. And tax the recipients of the payback at that very moment in time.

Forget about wanting to please the "markets" so they could buy more bonds. The next target will be to not issue any more bonds.

The ECB has not yet (by august 2012) wanted to acknowledge that, nor have the Germans who wield big influence there.

But it is a fair offer from us all to the bondholders, since they will see a lot of their money back, even if some of it may get eroded by inflation or taxes.

It is also a fair offer to us all, as while saving the bondholders and relieving the debtors we will avoid a total crash of the economy.

We are not far away from such a crash, which would be drowning companies, banks, debtors in a sea of debt, with no activity generating cash to pay for it, and bondholders getting nothing anymore.

Potilical systems would hardly survive such a series of events, so the proposal gives the wider population a continued chance of making its living, and protects bondholders, politicians, bankers of all sorts from being lynched.

Important note: The moment of buying up the sovereign bonds is also the moment to severely tax their holders. If you miss that moment, you will just increase the size of the financial cloud.

Unfortunately, that is just what is happening now (Oct 2012).

One important aspect of Ludwig Erhard's successful restart of the German economy was the fact that at the same time as introducing the new Deutsche Mark (DM), he erased most of whatever value holdings of the old ReichsMark (RM) still had, and above all whatever value debts protracted in the old RM had.

So Germany was allowed to restart on a pretty blank sheet, there were no rents on capital anymore, and everybody had to go out and do some work.

23. The way out: systemic changes : Proposals IV

Humans will always try to save for a rainy day, for future investments, or simply to feel freer. It makes no sense to go against that desire.

Let us assume a 10 % savings rate, which takes 10 % of our money out of circulation. Every month.

In order to keep activity high, a new influx of money-no-debt of the same size is needed. Every month.

Who should be the prime beneficiary of that ?

Banks? Governments? Military ? Public servants ? The education system ? Financiers ? Stockholders ? Bond holders ?

Since the system belongs to all of us, my vote is for every citizen to benefit from that, equally, throughout the solidarity zone (country, region, EuroZone)

Who should give out the cash ? The central bank, directly to the citizen, no intermediaries to siphon percentages off.

Any savings accumulation beyond one (?) year's salaries will be subjected to wealth taxes, in order to uphold the circulation of money.

Proposals
- central banks belong to the citizens of the country, or in our case of the Euro-Zone
- central bank has to learn how to generate money-no-debt (MND)
- only central bank is to be allowed to create, be it money&debt (MD) or money-no-debt (MND)
- commercial bank lends out money that it has, does not create any
- central bank ensures adequate supply of money&debt (MD) into the banking system
- central bank ensures there is an adequate supply of money-no-debt (MND) in the system

to do that:
- central bank creates new money-no-debt (MND)
   - o by distributing to each of its citizens (MND) to reflect and sometimes support real economic activity
   - o money-no-debt (MND) distributed according to country GDP, +/- some compensation

- finance ministry ensures enough money stays in the real economy system, and
- finance ministry severely taxes the cloud finance economy system
- finance ministry ensures taxes & public spending are aligned
- **no lending between banks** (avoid confusion, Libor & Euribor frauds, Domino effects)
- avoid parallel worlds of finance generating bubbles based on cash from sovereign debts …
- tax the finance cloud and trim it towards a reasonable size with respect to M3 & GDP
- break all high margin monopolies to avoid the build-up of another cloud with their monopolist rents

- the party has lasted long enough

- follow the advice of Ludwig Erhard,
    the only economist turned politician who really generated a miracle,
    and was brave enough to face down special interests in the interest of the social market economy;
    by doing that, he pulled all of Germany out of poverty, and put all Germans into a job
productivity benefits need to be shared with customers & employees, not concentrated on profits

On top of that, in the current european situation, a bit of european industrial & economic policy:

- **Get people in weaker EuroZone countries back to work by exporting factories to Spain, Greece, Portugal etc**
    - rather than to China, or
    - rather than importing workers from those same countries to northern Europe and expand factories there

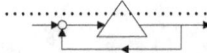

24. Debt & Interest

People with money will always succumb to the temptation to enslave people with none, with pleasure, just as drug dealers will always like to keep addicts well addicted so that they can suck out all their available cashflow & wealth.

As Tennessee Ernie Ford had it in "sixteen tons" :

> "Another day older and deeper in debt
> Saint Peter don't you call me 'cause I can't go
> I owe my soul to the company store"

This gets even more interesting when interests come in, especially since (unpaid) interests have the mathematical tendency to go exponentially haywire.
Sylvio Gesell a hundred years ago, and Prof Bernd Senf today insist on interest being the gravedigger of any economic system that uses it.
Well aware of the problems that arise from it, the Catholic Church banned lending out for interest in its earlier days, as did Islam.

The Catholic Church changed its mind later on, Islam did not, so that islamic finance now can now teach us a trick or two.

Personally, I think that MM Gesell & Senf are right, but I also think that banning interest has as much chance of success as the prohibition of drugs & alcohol, the banning of prostitution, or of freedom of speech.
My vote is to not prohibit interest, but to continuously lessen its impact by generating more money-no-debt (MND) and less money-debt, by replacing the money vanishing into the cloud with fresh MND, by keeping the amount of money around larger than the debt around.
M3 > D3 !!
Interests on bonds should not be fixed but depend on business success, bonds should be forcibly converted to equity if the going gets rough.
And income based on interests to be adequately taxed.

25. The value of money

Money in our pocket represents probable purchasing power that we have not yet exercised.
Once we have exercised it, it is gone. Somewhere else. If we decide to use it to pay back our debt, to the bank, it vanishes altogether.

So we tend to give it a lot of thought before spending it, unless we really need or want something now, and we can pay for it now.
In order to eliminate the "probable" in the sentence above, historically, people always wanted their money to be really worth something, and wanted to have that guaranteed.

After coming a long way down the ages with gold and silver standards, we now have paper (or rather: computer) currencies disconnected from any "real" thing.

That is a good thing, as we would not appreciate uncontrolled inflation just because somebody found a new large goldmine, or deflation just because a boat loaded with gold has sunk, or because the US Federal Reserve pulls back its gold from Germany (1929), thus spreading the depression around.

The quantity of money out there (in circulation) needs to reflect the size of economic activity it has to support, not the quantity of gold in the vaults.
The value of money is defined by the value we citizens see in it, not more, not less.
If I can buy my beer for 2,5 Euro, I do believe in the value of the Euro, and will continue to accept my salary being paid in it.
If the pub owner does not believe in the Euro anymore, then I can't pay for my beer, so I will not accept it either anymore.
If tomorrow the pub owner thinks he needs 3 Euro, I might go to another pub, or I might after a few more pubs confirm inflation, pay what it costs, then ask for a pay raise, as I lost 20% of the confidence I had in our money.

So the value of money, or rather our opinion about its value, is always defined by the quantity that we see circulating, and the goods & services that we see it buying.
Going back to gold or silver will not solve any problem, only add a few serious one's more.

Since the quantity of money should reflect the size of the economy it supports, it might be wise to increase the quantity that circulates by a few % each year, to give the economy a chance to grow by that same percentage. It the economy responds by increasing GDP, or "output", by the same percentage, perfect.
If it responds by the same % as inflation, bad luck, or poor job. The truth will be somewhere between the two, which is fine.
So let the finance minister and the central banker worry about having the nominal amount of money that circulates rise in a manner that compares well to then expected or wanted GDP growth, and let the economy make the best out of this fast-forward pass.
But use Money-no-Debt (MND) for the increase, do not create more problems by adding to somebody's debt.

26. *The quantity of money, and its circulation*

At any moment in time, the quantity of money circulating in an economy is whatever it is, if it is relatively stable, and if its velocity is quite stable as well, people and other economic actors have time to adjust to any internal changes, and mostly do so.

It gets more interesting when the quantity of circulating money changes, or if the velocity changes, or both.

If **one day**, many savers decide to spend more of their money, that will bring back a lot of cash into circulation, and generate extra demand:
- where this new demand hits scarce resources, prices will go up
- where it hits underused capacity, real GDP will go up to the benefit of everyone, with prices stable
- where it hits well-used capacity, prices will go up until capacity is extended by new investment or labor, to the eventual benefit of everyone

If the change in demand is too abrupt, like in the case of a big inflow/outflow of foreign money, prices will go up much quicker than anything else can reasonably adjust to, thus generating chaotic inflation in either the real economy, or in the exchange rate.
This has the potential to put this country's industry out of market and out of business from one day to the other. In that case, capital controls and/or serious exchange rate intervention would be a must on the borders of the economic/currency zone.

The Swiss have been playing the exchange rate since 2011, as they want to protect their export economy in the face of a general flight from Euro and US $ into Swiss Franc.
Malaysians protected their economy from the Asian Finance Crisis in 1998 by quickly reintroducing capital controls, despite plenty of contrary advice from FMI & others. As Dr Mahathir, the then Prime Minister and founder of modern Malaysia, saw how foreign lenders put all his neighbors into crisis by suddenly not wanting to roll over the debts anymore, he avoided financial problems by closing down the border for capital, keeping the money inside, until things would calm down.

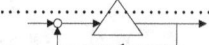

No one was hurt. Malaysia prospered. Bondholders had in the end little reason to complain.

If it all happens within the same economic zone, even internal capital controls might be necessary to stabilize a local economy.

No one should be allowed to rock the boat in manner that it will capsize and sink, so any force strong enough to do that will have to be identified, named, responsibilized, restrained, neutralized, maybe broken up. That statement counts especially for actors in the global financial cloud, which is much bigger than the amount of money circulating in the real economy, and therefore has to be disciplined in a way that it creates no real havoc.

If on **another day**, people and companies decide to spend less and save more, the fall in demand will lead to:
- where it hits previously scarce resources :
    prices going down (which may be positive overall ...)
- where it hits previously well-used capacity :
    underused capacity, again leading to
    lay-offs, less worker income to spend,
        dangers on the mortgage side;
    less company income and profit,
        dangers on the corporate bond side
    less tax income,
        dangers on the sovereign budget and bond side
- where it hits previously expanding capacity:
    stalled investment, leading to
    lay-offs in the equipment industry,
    with similar consequences as above

In mathematic principle, prices and wages of everything should quickly come down to match the missing nominal demand, and enable the same real demand to keep activity stable.

But that process has hardly ever been observed, as most prices do not come down easily, if at all.

Here a list of sticky one's:
- nominal (and real) wages
- mortgages
- interest on private debt
- interest on bonds contracted before

on top of that,
- people and companies will try to pay back debts, thus pulling out even more money from the circuit
- frightened banks will hardly lend out new money, thus avoiding money pulled out to be replaced

Irving Fisher states that with more and more money missing in the circulation, every dollar gets more valuable than before, and does so even faster than debtors are repaying their debt, an unsustainable situation that ends in disaster for everyone

These situations can get out of hand, Mr Fisher sees the system like a boat that cannot set itself upright anymore, and capsizes.

These situations do not have to get out of hand, the financial system (central bank & finance ministry) have the moral obligation to avoid serious trouble, to bring the boat back to level, to keep circulation of money alive, and keep it evolving (slowly upwards ?) in a more or less stable way.

How should they do that ?

27. Managing future crises

First, and above all, avoid pro-cyclic activities, like in a crisis

- reducing government outlays
- raising interest rates
- increasing reserve requirements on commercial banks
- increasing tax levels on consumption, and on "normal" salaries

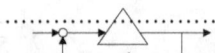

John Maynard Keynes was in favor of government deficit spending in such cases.

That has the advantage in keeping circulation up, but the disadvantage of increasing sovereign debt, which today is more than high enough just about everywhere.

Whether the government would spend the money wisely or not is not the subject of this chapter, but up to political debate and administrative efficiency.

Second, my vote would be to:

- Keep government expenses constant (not expanding, except for unemployment benefits)

- Bring down interest rates, but not to zero

- Keep reserve requirements stable

- Keep tax rates stable on consumption, and on "normal" salaries

- Increase taxes on financial clouds: wealth, savings, financial transactions, dividends, bond & other rents

- **Central bank to hand out fresh money-no-debt (MND) to citizens in order to stabilize demand**
  without increasing sovereign debt, and without fattening the financial cloud right away

and:
- stabilize balance of payments versus the rest of the world,
             to make sure money created at home translates into
             more money circulating at home

This last point may not be very easy to handle, and may or may not run against achievements of the European Union, and of globalization and will deserve another discussion.

It is easier when you still have a currency that can fluctuate and compensate for differences.

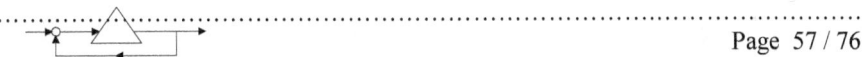

28. Politics

The goal of politics and economics should be to enable all of us to lead a free & decent life.

Whether free & decent lives can actually be achieved by all or most of us is another manner, but the systems we live in should at least not make it deliberately impossible, nor stand in the way.

It is interesting to see that while we all like to enjoy the fruits of economic liberalization and activity, we have a hard time accepting the rough side of it when it comes to worker or environment exploitation, unemployment, misery for most coupled with plenty for the few, and so on.

Marx & Engels, unions, socialism, communism, social-democratism have all tried to harness the ugly flowers of liberalism, and introduced new and sometimes worse problems while doing so. Even national socialism first thrived on the social results of the great depression, and on its liberal treatment.

Hot and cold war victories over some of these secondary problems have defeated only those, but have not solved the initial problem they wanted or at least pretended to solve.

That problem remains, it is still ours to solve, or at least ours to manage in a decent manner while we are around.

If the target is a decent life for us all, while accepting a better life for achievers, and a luxurious life for some over-achievers, an engineer's easy feed-back measurements on the system performance could be the local success of the luxury industry, and the amount of beggars in the street at the same time.

It should however be easy to find other indicators for the same purpose.

If both luxury and beggars go up simultaneously, time to do something about

      high-margin trusts, monopolies, taxes   on one side,

and

      local job content, pay levels, education,
      money-no-debt distribution   on the other side

If however the target is a good life for those who have a good life and/or good connections, then liberal economic principles are just fine, as money will eventually flow towards one narrow set of directions, while debt & misery will flow to the other, wider horizons.

With that in mind, let us look what we have been doing for the last generation, and think about what we want to do next.

29. Political Parties

It is the author's observation over many decades that there are 4 types of political parties that have transcended the "Big Man" concept and thrive on rational ideas rather than on individual strong-(wo)men.

One idea is to make sure that those who are doing well today will also do well tomorrow; that is the conservative (right as opposed to left) side of the spectrum.

That might be "fine" (?) if everybody was reasonable well off, which however is rarely the case.

Examples are conservative parties like the Tories in the UK, Republicans in the USA, Forza Italia (Berlusconi) in Italy, successive Gaullist parties in France.

Another party's goal is to make sure that those who are working well are also doing well, a domain that should be occupied by liberal parties in Europe like FDP in Germany, democratic party in Luxembourg, Lib-Dem's in the UK, but this type of party is never very strong as even good workers/earners recognize that they might be doing worse in some future, and might need organized help at that moment in time.

The third type of party wants to see everybody doing reasonably well, or at least have a chance of doing well, so that is obviously the domain of socialist and social-democratic parties in Europe, and the Democrats in the USA.

The fourth major type of party wants to preserve the environment, as green parties all over Europe can testify.

In order to gather votes, one party often goes beyond its original stand and picks up ideas from the others, with the result that it often seems difficult to tell one from the other.

Many parties are connected to a religion, in Europe mostly Christian Democrats can be cited as examples, they are mostly based on the

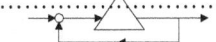

conservative parties' ideal to keep things as they are and under control, while addressing the most glaring poverty by charity work.

My disrespect goes for the organizations that aim at the well-being of the well-being, whole ensuring misery for the rest.

30. Religions

Religions create links between people and sometimes institutions, they offer a common value system , and a system of do's and don'ts, of duties and sometimes also of rights.

Important aspects are their tolerance towards other religions, and towards those who want to quit. These days, Islam for example is not doing well on these accounts.

Another important aspect is whether they start from the principle that we are all equal, or whether some are more equal as in George Orwell's "Animal Farm". Hindus are not doing well in this respect.

Does the religion readily embrace violence, or even promise a better life after death if you wage war here and now ? Again, Islam looks troublesome here.

The proclamation of human rights has set a good standard for the individual people's rights, but it is not complemented by a set of duties. So it does not replace religions, but leaves open important spaces for those.

Life after death should not be discussed here, but it is interesting to see what kind of behavior derives from one religion or the other, and what the economical consequences are.

Praying to God is effective in that it soothes your soul, may allow you to concentrate on a subject, but gods and saints can not be relied upon to influence what happens to us, and around us.

From all the gods that have been adored throughout history, the sun has proved the most reliable, as it comes back every day and heats us up, it so really makes a difference every day.

From all the saints that we pray to within the Catholic Church, Santa Claus is the most useful and reliable, he comes up once per year and is really good to us.

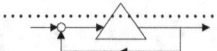

It means that most of us can really rely upon our parents, and that as parents we really are reliable. But don't count on gods or saints to bend the future your way, that is still your own job.

The author sees godly behavior in all of us when we do something good, and God representing the sum of all good. By contrast, the devil is then the sum of everything bad we do.

The protestant work ethic has made a big difference in the world, as it established and honored the value of hard work, and respects its results.

That is a big contrast to the standing of work in ancient Greece, to meditation in Buddhism, to the violent part of Islam, to the Hindu class system, to the catholic respect of hierarchies priestly and worldly, to Confucians' tendency to revere (and obey) their elders.

Religions that do not challenge the worldly powers of the land can last a long time, and can supplement the regime very well in keeping the population under control. Historically, problems then arise when the regime goes after the priests, but much less so when it goes after the folks.

Most religions offer reasonable value systems, often based on holy books, but also allow their priests to attain positions of power, through their license to interpret the holy books.

That power is regularly abused, and has been so for millennia.

Martin Luther translated the Bible into German, so that common folks could read it themselves. He thus broke the interpretation monopoly of the Catholic Church.

So the author appreciates the holy books, although some of them may not be very coherent, but is wary of the people who walk around with the books under their arm, telling us that they alone can correctly interpret them, and telling us what to do and what not.

Since they can fall back on ancient scripts meant to rule us forever, they tend to deflect anything new or different that does not fit their power structure.

Instead of updating their religion to fit the times.

Under these circumstances, the world is still quite flat in many places.

31. Southern European Countries : a managerial challenge

Although they have mostly failed miserably in the monetary and financial arena, the countries of Northern Europe give a better show of administrative discipline than some southern countries and regions, where the quality of governance has been found wanting over time.

All too often, administrations are expected to serve individual clients, rather than serving what might be called the common good.

All too often, politicians serve as "job"-providers, as credit facilitators for "job-creating" follies, efforts which tend to target some individual's income rather than actual meaningful work.

Only so much of that can be shouldered by an economy before it loses out, so this whole game needs to be changed.

But since politicians' minds only reflect their voters' minds, and are mostly not much better or worse than those, we have to acknowledge that mentalities are in for a big change, which may take some time. That is a managerial task, which requires understanding, emphasis, firm niceness, perseverance and stamina, and probably money as well.

Much is made of non-inference and non-interference, but in any larger company the manager of a poorly functioning department would be exchanged, replaced by someone with experience and so far not connected to the people in this workplace.

So the import of boring but able bureaucrats may be a business model for the political future in countries that need to progress. There have been excellent examples of this kind throughout history, let us note that Louis XIV's most effective prime minister, Mazarin, came from Italy.

In the end, being not-competitive is not a long-term option, we all have to learn to hold our ground in the open economical world.

So while devaluations have saved a lot of countries before, the central bank may save us once now, but it cannot and will not do that in a repeated manner. We all have to progress as well, and pay our own way again.

And above all, our governments at any level should not again spend more money than they get in. If we have a bridge to build, let us pay for it as we build it.

32. Business Margins

As passionate businessmen, we continuously (should) strive to increase our product's quality, attractiveness, innovation level, and of course the margins that we obtain. If one of us gets very successful in this last category, he gets rich and enjoys a well-filled bank-account, perhaps earning more money than he wants to or even can reasonably spend. Isn't that what we all would like to achieve?

Let us examine the other side of this coin, let us see what the effect on the wider economy is, if I get really rich thanks to the super-product or service that I just introduced, and that I can sell at a price that is good for me.

Competition hardly exists, or its product is not as "sexy".

Well, let us say that last year I made 1,1 ME that way, compared to the usual 0,1 ME of the years before.

I now set 1 ME more aside in the bank, and I do not know how to spend it, the bank doesn't know either, so the million just sits there.

Let's assume an average salary is 50 000 E per year, then I have taken out 1000 000 / 50 000 = 20 jobs out of the economy. Almost 2 per month.

Too bad for the others, why should I care, at long last I have my million, and there are more to come over the next years.

So the calculation is not too bad for 1 ME extra, but how about 1 BE? In that case I take 20 000 people out of work.

Let us now assume 50 000 $ as average salary in the US.

The reports have it that Apple, the most admired company of the day, sits on a cash hoard of about 100 billion $ (B$) by early 2012.

So Apple alone has put $100 \times 10^9 / 50 \times 10^3 = 2 \times 10^6 = 2$ million people out of job.

And it does so every time it sells a product where it enjoys the high margin that we businessmen all admire, as the price paid does not represent a lot of labor but a lot of profit.

So this round of money circulation turns out poorly for the labor market.

But, as long as they are sitting on their cash, the Apple folks are not putting the cash back to circulation, so the next round does not happen at all, or maybe only years later. Or the cash joins the financial cloud where it helps to blow up one bubble or another.

So, it does not come as a surprise if these days, american companies are hoarding cash from their profits in numbers rarely seen before, while the job market in America continues to struggle along.

What is strange after that is to see that most analysts look intensely at the state of the labor market every day, week, or month, at the same time as they look at the stock exchange.

What I do not understand is that the stock exchange comes down when the job market gets worse.

If I read through the few lines above, the job market gets worse often because profits go up.

Could it be that some analysts realize that with more and more people not able to pay for the goods, profits will disappear as well.

Could it be that there is a feedback loop between the reduction of the number of potential clients and the economy's worse-being ?

That feedback loop is pro-cyclic, capable of virtuous and vicious circles. So if things are let to themselves and they get worse, they get really bad after that. But if things improve, with more people in decently paid jobs, things will get much better.

So, reduction in margins will tend to improve the circulation speed of money, and its job-creating effectiveness.

Every time business margins in general are rising, the logical result is more people out of job.

If with greater competitive pressures, margins are receding, the job market goes up.

So if the goal is decent jobs and incomes, let us make sure there is enough competition around, so that margins, profits, job losses through the lack of circulating money are automatically limited. Welcome to the trustbusters.

If the goal is making sure I can keep my hard-won margin, make my millions or billions for as much as the market can bear, in the name of freedom and liberty, then leave me the freedom to wreck the job market at the same time. At the same time as I do that, I can boast about the X people that I do employ, and that their jobs would be in danger if my company hits competition or is broken up by the trust-busters.

I do not have to care about the many other people that I put out of their job by not allowing more money to circulate and pay for activity. Nobody knows these people, they are anonymous, they fill the job

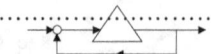

centers, they are spread around the country or around the world, they do not have an effective lobby.

But I can afford an effective lobby, and I have one.

Trust busters must be strong and represent the interests of the common good, as they have to fight against the interests of the existing business powers.

Much is made about the need to improve margins so that we have money left to do more investment.

Alas, it takes much longer for a company to decide about an investment and then to do it, than it takes for consumers to just spend the money. Thus the speed of circulation is lowered in the investment loop. Periods of high unemployment are not ideal for investment loops.

On top of that, and very importantly, only a fraction of the extra business income is really invested in new products, services, capabilities, plants, capacity, quality etc, as most of it seems to land in the financial cloud.

Some of it is invested into productivity, generating higher margins and more unemployment, at least until the margins have normalized under competitive pressure.

33. Productivity

It may not always seem so, but there is progress in our skills, knowledge, ways to work etc, so we are all, or at least most of us most of the time, getting better & faster, when doing our work. That helps quality, and productivity.

Increased productivity within a company means

a) much more income for more expenses, when business is growing fast

b) more income for the same expenses, when business is growing

or

c) same income for less expenses, when business is stable

or

d) less income with even lesser expenses, when business is receding

Sometimes we read machine cost for expenses here, most of the time we however read labor "cost" or the size and cost of the workforce.

While

(a) and (b) describe the happy situation when our business is growing, and our bottom line grows even faster, when we are happy to keep or even expand our workforce and pay it well, but, to be noted, our margin goes up, as less of our selling price is covered by actual work, paid work

situation (c) is a lot different, as here in order to reap the benefits of our productivity gains, we have to shed some of our workforce, business not growing at least as fast as our productivity advances

situation (d) is still worse, recession hits our business, and we slash the workforce even faster than revenues drop

(c) and (d) are the same in this respect: our margins go up as we have slashed the workforce faster than revenue drops, so again, our selling price is covered by less work than it used to

If competition is tough, the increased margins do not hold up for long, and will get back to a lower level.

We may not be calling our former employees back, but at least by lowering the margin, we have liberated the extra money so that our customers could in addition to our product buy some more of the same or from another product line, increasing demand there and directly generating work, now.

If competition is not too much of a problem, we keep the increased margins for the company's purposes, but unless we immediately spend it on some consumption, investment or higher salaries for all or for some, we have destroyed this month's jobs by eliminating the demand for them.

We have lengthened the queues at the job center.

Or, in an economy with full employment, we have liberated workforce that can now better be employed somewhere else, and will have an easy time finding this other spot.

Personally, unless we are in a full employment situation, it does make no macro-economical sense to push productivity and lay off people.

Best practice is to get to full employment first, and do productivity after that.

34. Growth & Environment

A lot has been written on the limits to economic growth, starting with the Club of Rome in 1972. It is clear that if more economic activity automatically means more natural resources, more pollution, more nuclear risk etc, and then growth cannot be eternal.
But it does not have to be that way:

Growth can be defined as the % increase of GDP, and since GDP is the sum of our salaries

Growth is the % increase of the sum of our salaries, and there is no direct link to using up natural resources
The only resource that at the minimum gets used, is our own time and effort, that effort may be intellectual, or manual, or both
So, the service and knowledge societies that we are evolving towards may not weigh so heavily on the environment, even if the whole world's population picks up a paid job.
The other side of this hopeful coin is that activities with clear links between growth and natural resources need to be watched, and a serious tax, or some other limitation, has to be put on the use of those resources

35. Unions

Even if most companies do probably not agree, it is certainly beneficial for any company's management to have somebody to talk to while managing the quality of the workplace, and of work. That somebody, indeed the whole employee council, should be elected in free, secret elections within the company, and/or the site.
Care has to be taken that unions are not getting into a position where they can blackmail the company in order to pull too much of the linen to their side. Unions should be partners in management, and not behave like monopolists. In the US, not only companies have been broken up in the name of trust-busting, but also unions.
The French have a nice couple of words that says " droits acquis", or vested rights, vested interests. It means that whatever social (?) vested right we have won in the past, is there to stay with us forever.
Unfortunately, a vested social right is always also a vested economic right, and a vested economic right does not exist.

In french: « un acquis social est toujours un acquis économique, mais un acquis économique n'existe pas ».

Economic success today does not guarantee economic success tomorrow, and can therefore not guarantee (labor and other)contracts based on that assumption.

If you want to keep your "droits acquis ", as an employee you better help the company or your economic environment to prosper so that largesse can be earned, and its redistribution thus enabled. And that might even mean giving up on some of the "droits acquis" in order to help your economy, and fight with the company and not against it.

The company itself has to value this kind of contribution as well.

Salary indexation does lead to immediate inflation in a booming economy, as higher salaries are immediately transformed into higher prices. If competition is harsh, if customers are picky, it may lead to prices staying the same and margins going down, in the light of the discussion on margins that will lead to more employment if the extra money is spent.

Unless the company itself cannot absorb this margin degradation as it has not built up its productivity over the year, and gets into trouble.

It is probably best if wages are negotiated on a company by company basis, with cost of living increases an important part of the available information. The other important bit of information being the state of the company's finances and their outlook, shared in an honest manner with the union delegates.

Widespread progress is needed on honesty here.

To go with Ludwig Erhard, pay raises should be vastly influenced by productivity raises over the year, in nominal currency terms that include inflation. If a company cannot afford a raise this year, you are free to either accept that as a matter of fate, or try harder for more company success next time, or go out and work for another company.

If management tries to fool you (i.e. the delegation), make that well-known, and go on strike until the responsible managers are exchanged.

If you feel that management is poor and everyone is suffering from that, go out and work somewhere else, or have the union buy enough shares, get on he company board and improve management. By then however, you might be poor managers yourselves....

36. Taxes

We all have the tendency to enjoy whatever the state does for us, and complain about what he does not or what he does not "well" enough.

At the same time, our asymmetric mindset enables us to avoid paying taxes as much as possible.

Taxes are for most of us our only direct contribution to the state's work, leaving it all to the others is a negative sum game and the state may be able to do even less, and worse. Also for us. So let us relearn to be responsible citizens, let us grow up again, and help each other along the way.

In the field of taxes, the principle of each according to his possibilities is quite sound, if you have more income and/or more wealth, you should pay more. Nobody should pay none.

Personally, I am in favor of simple rules and of avoiding just about all exceptions, of a tax code that fits well into a few pages, and of an implementation that does not need to keep armies of accountants and lawyers busy.

Government, parliament, or society, need to agree on some basic aspects like target % of GDP for taxes (and social security), thus defining the size of the state with respect to the other actors.

At the same time, they should agree on the roles of the state, that is what to do with the money brought in by taxes, and what not.

Changing your opinion drastically every few years will not help, countries with a reasonable consensus on these points that live by it for a generation or so will come out better than others, who might lose a lot of efficiency by deciding back & forth.

The US is a negative example these days, as there seems to be no agreement about what to do, so energies are lost fighting each other rather than building a reasonable future.

If you collectively decide that taxes should make up say 40 % of GDP, the easiest way is to tax everything the same way.

If you find that is not socially just, you can invent a curve where the % tax goes up with income.

37. Capitalism, Creditism, Debtism

We have seen that within our current system there is more debt than money to go around, that we have no net capital at all but net debt.

At the same time, we all think we live in a capitalist system, and most of us do not mind.

For good or bad, things have however evolved in a direction where it is mostly not existing capital that moves the economy, but credit from the bank.

For example, Mr. Lakshmi Mittal

has been able to buy Arcelor, the big steel company, not with the capital he might have saved before, but with the credit that he got from the banks that supported (or demanded ?) his move.

And those banks created most of that money themselves, benefiting from loose reserve requirements as set by their central banks. Using real money, it is difficult to compete in such a situation when your opponent is able to use vast amounts of new virtual money, that will still count as legal tender.

So, cheap virtual credit that counts as real money makes the world go round these days, and is helpful in promoting all kinds of purposes, be they of economical, business, political, pork-barrel, societal or even criminal kind.

But the story does not stop there, as the credits described also generate debt. While everybody goes after the money so created, which usually ends up with the wiliest smarts, the associated debt is being pushed around until it ends up with the one who can defend himself the least.

In German we say: " wer behält den schwarzen Peter ?", or who gets stuck with black card ?

In the case of Arcelor-Mittal, it was the company itself that ended up with the debt on its books, and struggling to pay for it, by leaning on its people.

In the case of the company I worked for a few years ago, the debt contracted for the company's purchase also ended up on our books, with the company being sucked out of its wealth even before we had the chance to generate it. We were then an easy prey for the next crisis.

So we are really living in debtism, and the debt stays around, lingers on, and generates problems.

Let us get out of that mode!

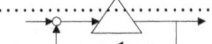

38. Freedom

Most of us are quite free, the question is,
            free from what,   and
            free to do what ?

Well,

I feel free when I

- can spend my money as I wish, spend my time as I want, with whom I want, where I want.

- can do what I want, within some reasonable limits, which are mostly set by others, but which I have accepted and do respect.

- can choose my education, (with some help from the old folks), my occupation or my job, and when I can change my job if it suits me.

- can vote for the candidate(s) that I prefer, or set myself up as candidate if I think I would do a better job

- feel secure, when no one comes to bug me, threaten me, rob, hit, wound or kill me.

- can aspire to "higher levels", (without necessarily getting there), with no law or strange practice standing in the way

- can choose my partner myself, or prefer to give it more time and choose later or not at all

- can sign the contracts that I want (even when they are limiting my freedom in certain areas after that ...)

- am not discriminated against, when my worries are of personal nature (these are bad enough ...)

- can choose my own religion, and leave it again when I want (the latter seems difficult with Islam)

- have not more debt than I can support

my freedom is limited by

- my duties towards my family, my friends
- my adherence to a religion and its do's and don'ts
- my respect for other people's religions (up to a point ?)
- my own set of values
- my respect for the environment
- my respect for coming generations
- my duties towards my employer, or my customers
- my duties towards my local community
    (neighbors, village, local taxes)
- my duties towards my wider community
    (country, continent, world, federal taxes)
- my duties towards my contract partners (banks ...)

and

- by the lack of financial resources
    to pay for all the things that I would like to do ...

Most of the freedoms are luckily guaranteed by the convention on human rights, although organizations like

    violence-based economic entities (Mafia ...)
    pseudo-religious sects (scientology, et al)

certainly make their best to deny us some of these, when we have the bad luck to find ourselves on their path.

In practice, two points are difficult to handle:

a) choosing a job so that I can make a living
b) avoiding the debt trap

a) For most of the last generation, finding a decent job was not easy, changing jobs because we did not like the last one was very difficult, as there have never been enough jobs around to allow a selection worth its name.

Having hired hundreds of people myself over the course of an industrial career, I can say that this has been an employer, not an employee market.

This aspect has severely limited my freedom over the years, and not only mine. But there simply were and are not enough jobs around.

b) My house was built with the help of a mortgage, so I was in debt for almost 20 years. The obligation to pay up every month is not a big problem as long as I can afford it, as long as job perspectives and health are ok.

Change either one of the last 2 points, and things may turn sour very quickly as the pressure of debt then comes on top of problems with health or job.

With a bit of bad luck, one problem compounds the other and I'm stuck.

Also, I may have bought a car on credit, and some household items as well …

No way to feel free in that context.

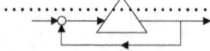

What to do ?

a) There has to be a bigger number and selection of jobs at any time: enough of the money has to circulate and keep circulating to support demand

and,

b) as debt is a clear antithesis of freedom, private household debt should be kept at a minimum, as well as interest on it

  => no predatory lending
  => no demand for additional collateral (less foreclosures)
  => only one credit card each, with limits appropriate
            to financial situation, and limits on interest
  => wide use of debit cards to handle expenses
  => overdebt situations to be handled by trusted authorities,
            evenhandedly between creditor & debtor interests

Now those things , and maybe a few more, would really help in getting us closer to the lands of freedom, with freedom for all, not only for a few.

After all, to quote Woody Guthrie again:

" This land is your land, this land is my land "